The DEVIL Has a SON

The 13th Step

WILLIAM AMOS HAGWOOD

NEWMAN SPRINGS PUBLISHING
320 Broad Street
Red Bank, NJ 07701

First originally published by Newman Springs Publishing 2023

ISBN 978-1-68498-375-9 (Paperback)
ISBN 978-1-68498-376-6 (Digital)

Printed in the United States of America

I, William A. Hagwood, do testify that every word and event are true. I give this truth to the world because of God's glory.

> Now, in this that I declare unto you
> I praise you not, that ye come together
> not for the better, but for the worse. (1
> Corinthians 11:17)

But for the worse, so knowing that things get worse before it gets better.

"The cost of sin is too high," so we experience with and observe facts or events, such as the seven deadly sins:

1. Lust, which is no. 1 of the flesh and for power.
2. Then envy, a desire to possess someone else's possessions
3. Pride, in that the victory was all yours with no help
4. Greed, a selfish desire to have that what we need—greedy
5. Wrath, extreme anger with the intent to do bodily harm
6. Sloth, laziness and too sorry to finish anything started
7. Gluttony, eyes bigger than our stomach, a habitual greed of excessive eating

The seven-headed dragon represents the seven deadly sins and is seven times more wicked than his father, the devil and has been born on the earth today. And there is only one possible help, the only hope.

"In the mighty name of Jesus," come into my life so that the wicked one's works will be destroyed.

An eternal question is, are you going to serve the Lord either the easy way or the hard way? In my early days, I preferred the hard way, not knowing that the easy way felt good.

Going to the Other Side

The Thirteenth Floor

In the year 1992, in the month of February, I, William Hagwood, was on the thirteenth floor of Grady Hospital in Atlanta, Georgia. "I was in a white struggle jacket."

I was being admitted into the psych ward to be evaluated and to determine if I had lost my mind. I was introduced to a young doctor that asked me what I saw and what happened. I said, "The devil had a son, which was a seven-headed dragon."

The young doctor stated to me, "You're going to be in the hospital for a very long time."

The chief physician would arrive at 7:00 a.m. to give a second opinion and stated, "From my viewpoint, I think you have lost your mind."

As I sat in a seat with a straight jacket on and being restrained, I thought about telling the doctors something different in the morning to get out of the situation. As I was sitting in a chair around other patients and clients, a patient grabbed a handful of pencils (about eight) and said to me, "I know who you are." Then he tried stabbing me with the pencils. With this straight jacket on, I was defenseless.

The male nurses restrained him and loaded him up with Thorazine. After an hour went by, he asked if he could get another shot of that. Many hours went by, and it was almost morning. I had my talk with God about telling the truth or lying. *Okay, God, I will tell the truth.* If I didn't know anything else at the time, I knew the truth would make you free.

At 7:00 a.m., the chief of the psych doctors came to me to evaluate me but stated, "Take that straight jacket off of this human being." And with that statement alone, I felt like telling this doctor the truth. He did not make me feel like I was out of my mind.

He asked, "What happened?" I told him that I had finished a pack-and-load furniture job with $320 from the driver and decided I was going to the boulevard to get high. I went to the corner store to buy some Mad Dog wine. Then I went to the boulevard to buy some crack and had fourteen rocks for $100. I was set, and all I needed was a room. On the boulevard was a new hotel, but they said that they had no vacant rooms.

I was persistent and wouldn't take no for an answer, so the desk clerk looking at me as if to say, "How bad do you want it?" and knowing what it was going to take, I made him an offer of an extra fifty dollars, so he said, "The room is under some construction."

I said, "Whatever," and he gave me the keys because I was in a hurry to get high. Now I had fourteen rocks for one hundred dollars and two bottles of the Mad Dog (MD) 20/20. My room number was 412 on the fourth floor of this new hotel, and everything looked great in the room, so I did not ask any questions.

What I knew was that I had this high coming and wasn't going to share. The question was why they didn't want anyone in this room Well, it is mine now, and let's get high. I opened a bottle and down the hatch. I then fixed my pipe and put on a whole-dime flame like Fire Marshal Bob. I brought the pipe down and waited. Nothing happened, so I said out loud, "These sons of bitches sold me some flex," but let me try this again with much more.

I put on a whole-dime piece. I turned a fifth of the Mad Dog (MD) 20/20 first because this was a big one. I brought fire to the pipe like Godzilla fighting King Kong and said, "Look out, Mother, here comes that man."

The lights went out, and I thought that I died and went to hell. Then my eyes opened, and there was someone in my room. It was Al, a friend that I knew and trusted. I asked Al what he was doing in my room and how did he get in because the door was locked from the inside.

Action Speaks Louder than Words

Al said that he was here for the birth of the child. "What child?" I asked, and for what reason is this happening in my room? Al stated that this room was reserved for the birthing of the son of the devil. I ran out of the door and down the hallway and into an elevator. I went to the first floor to see the desk clerk and tell him what was going on.

I came to him with a sense of urgency to stop the madness. I told him what Al had stated to me about the birth of the devil's son. The clerk's comment was that the management knew. I said first, "What happened to the other desk clerk?" The clerk that was there told me that he was appointed at this time for the birth of the child.

I thought, *There can only be a few things going on here. Either I'm trapped in the adversary of the devil or I have been hagged.* I am on the other side, trapped and can't get free. I have heard about being on the other side of the wall of time, but I don't know that this is it because of the imps. They're agents of the underworld or hell.

I started on my way back to my so-called room. For some reason, the hallway had gotten longer, miles longer. It took me thirty minutes to make it to the elevator, and it took the elevator another twenty minutes before getting to the fourth floor. The hallway went around and around.

It took me another hour to get to my door, and where was everyone? No one was in the hotel but me and whatever was in my room. I opened the door, and there it was. This was messed up, and I could see the child was mad. I have never seen anything so disgusting in my life.

The child looked like a bat in his face, was black as coal, and has eyes like human eyes and no skin on and no bottom half. Because the child was born into this world and hell was his final resting place, he said, "I will be the reconstruction of hell." Al said to me, "He is the seven-headed dragon, and I will be here to watch him grow the seven heads, to be seven times more wicked than his father."

I ran out of the room to the elevator and down to the first floor to get someone to go to my room and stop the madness. I said to the desk clerk, "I am not going back to that room until you call the police." I demanded they call the law. So they came with a straightjacket, but before the officer took me away, I said, "I need to show you what's going on."

We went to the room to see what I was talking about, and when we got to the door, I said, "You won't believe what you're about to see." Then we opened the door, and nothing was there, so I looked around the room and under the sheets. The officer pulled his gun and said, "Hold it. Put your hands up, and you need to stay off of drugs."

The officer put me into this white straightjacket, and here I am. The psych doctors said to me, "And you can go, Mr. Hagwood." I ran back to the hotel because I had left $142 under the mattress. When I got back to the room and opened the door, there was a sheet twisted, looking like the child or the son of the devil.

There was a red crown on his head, a crown of blood. I looked under the mattress and got my money and left. For years after that, my friends or so-called friends called it a nightmare. I was still on drugs but in another dimension. I was scared to go to sleep because of the control over my body that the demons had.

It is hard for me to get any rest, and no one could sleep around me because the torment was too great, and my addition for crack cocaine got even worse. I was drinking and smoking on an average of $350 to $500 daily. The money that I had was just a starter. Most people addicted would say that they had a monkey on their back, but I have a seven-headed dragon that had more ideas than I could imagine.

On Peachtree Street in Atlanta, there was a shop that sold fake gold and would stamp the jewelry with 14K stamped on chains. I was looking like new money. So I would buy a good amount of fake gold pieces and dress up with them. I would go to the hood and spend some money with everyone looking at my jewelry.

They asked me how much. I would say, "It is no price for what my mommy gave me." I would let time go by and then would say, "I really don't want to because my mother got this for me on her birthday." Matter of fact, forget it, man. I can't do that. Then I would hear the magic.

It Wasn't Me

My birth name is William A. Hagwood, but my nickname was given to me by Rob Knox, which was "Nightmare." So I look back to the past only to never return to the "seven-headed dragon."

I must say that I was amazed with his power, planning, and trickery, and I myself couldn't think or do all the events in craftiness as myself. So I say, "It wasn't me." And the one thing that I would say every night is, "One day, the Lord is going to deliver me."

We had this saying from the school of hard knocks: "You've graduated." But it was to another level of darkness in bondage, in the wrong direction. If you don't believe that there are powers greater than ourselves, you won't believe anything that I am writing. Then I won't be covered by the blood, the blood of Jesus.

The problem was not knowing how to fight after being loyal to the seven-headed dragon. Shortly after my hotel episode, the appetite and adrenaline of the demon excited me in moments, the ideas that would come up, knowing that it wasn't me.

I had landed this driving job with "Georgia Peach" moving and storage and was introduced a seven-step plan in a satisfied move to Mr. Orland, the owner. Making a thousand dollars a truck, in slow season, sounded great to him because deception was Mr. Orlando's first name. He would later end up in prison for credit card fraud.

My home address was down a hill in a rooming house, which was a dope hole. Two other dope dealers live in the house with me, and I never wanted them to see me high or experience a "nightmare." I couldn't stand the way they talked about crackheads, which was their bread and butter. Anyway, one of their clients came over one day when no one was home, but he had a little bit of something and gave me a hit of it. And the dragon was loose.

I kicked their doors down and found drugs, alcohol, new clothes, etc. and the best thing was .357 Magnum with a pearl handle and gold and nickel plate. So we loaded up a couple of shopping carts, and down the road we went. Making it to the train station to the other side of town, I was the man with a plan.

I told many stories and lies, laughing until everything was gone. Then at about 2:00 a.m. when my high was gone and the devil, I got paranoid, and everywhere I looked, the boys were coming. To the right, I saw them, and toward the left also, I saw them.

So I run through some woods and down a hill across a big, wide road scared of being killed. I ran into this church yard and hid behind a dumpster. Then I heard this voice: "Are you tired?" I came from behind the dumpster, and there stood Pastor Cobb. He said, "Hide yourself in the chapel, and we'll figure out what to do with you in the morning."

The next day, I was placed in a basement of a ministry house because there was a $400 reward for my whereabouts. And Pastor James, knowing what was going on, said to Pastor Cobb, "This Will Hagwood is putting everyone in this ministry in danger. So I think that we need to eliminate him for safety reasons." Then Pastor Cobbs made this statement, which caused me to listen as my mentor, "It's a shame when you're scared of living and terrified of dying."

Pastor Cobb was my hero, and the following Sunday, he preached a sermon of my understanding on satanic powers and warfare and how things were in place with three heavens, how the second heaven was for the devil, and the only way for us to make it to the third is to go through the second. This made a lot of sense to me, but I was placed on a bus going to Texas.

I Have Graduated

I ended up in Dallas, Texas, with Pastor Cobb and staff with developed strength for the loss of drugs. And Pastor Cobb was a powerful preacher and teacher and popular in word! Then one day, I heard that Pastor Cobb was having a party. So I wondered what kind of party he pastor could have. I went to his apartment and saw two young boys. One was talking to me with his shirt off telling me that Cobb had bought a key of drugs and he was waiting for a turn with Cobb.

I had said in anger, "What the hell is happening?" I thought to myself, *My hero turned out to be a zero.*

So I ended up in the streets of Dallas at a hotel with seven floors and forty rooms to a floor. It was the biggest drug ring that I have ever seen. I had got a room next to a guy named Carlos, and he said that he didn't smoke drugs nor sell any drugs. But that turned out to be the biggest lie in Texas.

Carlos ran that hotel and many more. He also bought my room and paid me to leave the hotel. I ended up at a number of his locations, and he would also pay me to leave again. I earned the nickname "Mike Tyson" in Dallas and had graduated to a $500 habit a day.

Then one day, I ended up at Ms. Carletta's house, and everyone coming in and out had to pay me in drugs. So

Ms. Carletta had called Carlos to come and straighten me out. He came and set me down telling me all that he was going to do to me with his boys with him. He told me to not say a word, to just listen. When he was finished, everyone in the house was waiting on him to go upside my head.

But he said, "Here, take this pack, and don't ever come back to this woman's house again." It was an eight ball in my hands, and I turned so that everyone could see. I said to Carlos, "Never again will I come on the property." But on the other properties that Carlos had, it was the same thing. And at one location, I was double-teamed and made a vicious reputation that made everyone remember and talk about it.

"I had graduated."

So as time went on, the boys were tired of me and was planning on killing me, so I left that area and went to the south side.

On the south side, I would stand out in front of a drug dealer's house, a girl named Cookie, and would challenge for someone to come out and fight. Or give me a pack, and I will leave. So Puerto Rican Red came out with a hammer to fight. Little did Red know that this was what I was living for.

So we fought, and I was too fast for him, and little did everyone know that I was 1986 Open Gloves champ out of Huntsville, West Virginia. I threw twenty-punch combinations, and the dragon in me had become more vicious than before. But regardless of that, whenever I was tired and needed to rest, someone would always open their door, and in the morning, I was grateful.

Then one morning on the south side, I wondered what I was going to do for a fix. I guess I was tired, and then came "Big Chubby" with two girls on his arms. He said to me, "Look at that bitch nigga." I jumped off of the third step of the house I was at into Chubby's mouth.

Chubby was 6'3" at about 310 pounds with a handful of rocks that he had bullied Mama for. And after that whipping that I put on Chubby, I had become Mama's hit man. She fed me crack day and night because she liked me, like if the sun couldn't get any brighter, but I think that she enjoyed watching me fight with vicious anger.

Then on a Thursday morning at about six on a hill, Hercules sold me some Buddha Dean. And it was about principle because at the drug house Cookie run, her brother, Rick, fed me drugs not to fight him. But in my heart, I think it was about who was the king of the hill on the south side.

And Chubby would jump up and down knowing that this was going to be something to see. So for two days, I waited for Hercules on the hill, and everyone fed me drugs knowing how vicious and violent it makes me.

Then came Hercules after two days, and he was saying something, but I had no words for him. I threw the best uppercut that has ever been thrown that sent Hercules in a flip. Then I jumped on him, not giving him any air to breathe. And as I was on top of him, he bit me. He took a mouthful of flesh out of my chest that had me screaming. Then that got him up off the ground.

And when he got up, he has a red brick in his right hand, smashing it against the left side of my head. He smashed that brick against my head three times, and it made me mad. I roared at Hercules like if I was saying, "Is that all you have?"

He dropped the brick and ran. Then the crowd told me to run to the fire station. But I yelled, "I'm the king of this hill, and no one can do anything about it!" and as I walked down the hill, blood was coming down my face. I looked then saw Hercules coming with a gun. So I started running toward the fire station and was almost there when a city bus pulled in front of me.

The driver was stopping at a bus stop, and I stopped him. I got on the bus shouting, "HE GOT A GUN!" and no more was needed to be said. The driver pulled off in a hurry then asked me if I need to go to the hospital. I said, "What does it look like?" So I went to the hospital with a concussion. But the good thing about it was, I didn't feel a thing when Hercules was smashing that brick against my head.

But Where, What, and Why

I ended up at a mission, some kind of disciples for Christ. And my intentions were to heal up before making any decisions because I had been out of my mind. And I needed to regroup and plan before moving from this location. The teaching was great, and for me, it was because of these topics:

> And the great dragon was cast out, that old serpent called the Devil and Satan which deceived the whole world; he was cast out into the earth and his angels were cast out with him. (Revelations 12:9)

> Therefore rejoice ye heavens and ye that dwell in them. Woe to the inhibitors of the earth and at the sea. For the devil is come down unto you, having great wrath because he knoweth that he hath but a short time. (Revelations 12:12)

So I started studying day and night from the front of the gospel to the back and reading different books about angels and demons plus books on the order of God and for what purpose God allowed things to happen and finding out that I had tapped into another entity between life and death.

The question was, for what reason was I there? I needed to find out, so I started with the beginning. And I found out that there are three parts to hell, and the last is a lake of fire.

After two months, I was asked to leave the ministry because I wasn't teachable or I was moving too fast. So I left the ministry and wanted to leave because I had made up my mind. At least, I thought so anyway. The calling was too great. The dragon and the devil had a calling like Dracula. My blood was required, and I couldn't break loose.

So I ended up on the eastside of Dallas, and everyone knew or heard of me. I was welcomed like the prodigal son and was asked where I was and what I have been doing. I had said that I was trying to change to stop this madness. But they said, "Tyson, you'll never stop smoking crack. You will smoke this shit till the day you die."

And I said, "The devil is a liar." *One day, the Lord is going to deliver me.* I don't know when, but I do know that that's the kind of God he is.

After having different people cash stolen checks for me that I had stolen from the drug dealers, I had to leave Texas. *Out of town wasn't far enough.* So I found out that there was this ministry called "Deeper Life" that was bussing members to Florida to see Bishop M. B. Jefferson. So I joined the ministry and said that I wanted to change and serve God.

So Bishop Williams put a bucket in my hand and said, "Go to work." But what do I say? Bishop Williams told me to ask God what to say. So I came up with "a penny for heaven." For every penny, I'll pray that your family member makes it to heaven. And I turned out to be a natural, and everyone would watch me preach on the highways with a bucket. I did $300–600 a day and was the bishop's favorite. Bishop Williams wanted to introduce me to Bishop M. B. Jefferson.

In Florida, I felt safe, away from a death sentence, and I'm leaving all the madness behind me. But little did I know that wherever I went, the madness came also. And before I knew it, I decided to find out what opportunities I had in Tampa, Florida, because I couldn't go back to Texas. But Bishop Williams did not receive that from me, and the only way that I could get my clothes out of his possession was to call the police.

So I ended up at The Good Samaritan, but there wasn't anything good about this place. This was a new kind of "New Jack City." And the theory that emphasized "if you can't beat 'em join 'em" was in effect. So down the street from The Good Samaritan was a drug dealer named Gee, and right off, he liked me. And he would give me a fifty pack for twenty dollars.

Super Bad

Bringing Gee's loyalty was a difference in respect that he already had for me. One day, he said to me, "Chris standing over there hasn't paid me my money." So Gee nodded his head for me to attack Chris, so I hit him with a twenty-punch combo. Then Gee's girlfriend screamed, "STOP IT! Look at what you did to Chris!" Chris was in bad shape with a broken jaw.

Gee had given me a hundred-dollar block that night or a yard. And later on, I found out by Chris that he only owed Gee twenty dollars. "It was about principle and respect" is what I told Chris. And not too long after that, Gee was locked up, so I ended up being a runner for Bean. He was a so-called "any and everything" pants down to his knees with three kids and Gee's girlfriend to play mother.

And Bean had promised me a package at the first of the year. But you know how that went, and I asked or reminded Bean, but he put a gun in my face while talking crazy to me. So I waited and waited until I was sure that Bean wasn't home and put my shoulder to his door. It was time to say Merry Christmas and ho ho ho.

I filled two bags up with toys and items then went to Jefferson Street to sell everything. I did so and was broke in the morning when Bean was looking for me. I was sleeping in The Good Samaritan when Frank came and told me that

Bean was making up a story about me being in his house. I said to Frank, because he was security, that I have been in this bed all night long with witnesses.

He said that he believed me and later asked me where I was going with a big bag of clothes. I said, "To the laundromat," but I was getting the hell out of dodge, looking for a bus stop out the back door. I ended up at the VA waiting on the shuttle bus for Orlando.

Pay to Play

I ended up at the Coalition in Orlando, which was a home-less shelter. For one dollar, you could sleep on a mat at night, and it was elbow to elbow, smelling like butt and feet. Then on the sides, front, and back of the building were drinking, smoking, fighting, buying, and all "the works of the devil."

I was in smoke heaven, and anything and everything go. Little did they know that in making up your own rules to play, I wasn't playing with a full deck. And the games I played were for keeps with the dragon coming up with some great stuff all day long.

Then I saw Red and Vern just getting in from the Florida Keys and had been working with FEMA. *And it was time to play.* So I said to Red, "Just give me a crumb, and I'll go away. PLEASE, MAN, I haven't had a hit all day." Then Red gave me a crumb, and I looked at it and said, "REALLY!" and smacked him with it.

Red then pulled a knife but made me mad, and he saw it. He dropped the knife and ran. Then Vern called for Red to double-team, but Red wanted no part of me. So I knocked Vern down a couple times and let him back on his feet, just having some fun, and then backed up telling Vern that I was getting tired.

Vern then connected a blow that broke my nose, and I was in so much pain that I was just holding my face. Then

I looked, and Vern was knocked out on the sidewalk about ten feet from me. I asked a friend or running buddy named New York what had happened, and he said, "That was the fastest." And it was so fast that I'm not sure if I really saw it. I told him I know because I'm not really sure that it was me.

Two guys had picked Vern up and carried him to a bench so that he could recover. Then the dealers and everyone around that was there gave me a piece of crack. My buddy, Mike, looked at me and said, "Your nose is crooked." I told him to take a hit. I looked at what was given to me, and it looked about a yard. Mike said, "Big Will, I think that you need to go to the hospital because your nose looks like its broken."

And I said, "Late," so Mike said, "Okay, let's get high."

Then early in the morning at about five when everything was gone, the pain came. The pain went from my nose to my brain or head that was so great that someone needed to call an ambulance. At the hospital, I had time to think about what really happened because I was taking credit for something that I didn't do.

Because I was holding my face in the greatest pain when my nose was broken, it must have been an angel that stepped in and knocked out Vern for me. *My mind, with that pain, was not on planet Earth.*

So after I had returned from the hospital, I had decided to go back to church. And I ended up with Pastor Glendy's at Harvest Baptist Church. They had a men's house, rent-free. Just service God and come to church.

I Can Fake It until I Make It

In 2002 at Harvest Baptist in the men's house, I shared a room with one brother. I said to myself, *I can fake it until I make*, and laugh at myself because the brother in my room was not faking it. He would get up every morning at five praying and praising then speaking in tongues to God. He says, "Hallelujah Lord to the highest praise, you are the only true God, King of kings, Lord of lords. YOU ARE MY EVERYTHING!"

I couldn't stand him, and it was because of the dragon that was in me versus the love of Christ that he had in him. And the bad thing about all of what happened between me and him was that I never asked or knew his name. And as time passed and the weeks went on, I was giving a donation to the church weekly from working at Atlantic Van Lines, fifty here to the church and seventy dollars also.

Then I started smoking crack that was right around the corner. I ended up at an old man's house that was the bike man because he supposedly fixed bikes for a living.

He also had rooms for rent and was a part-time pimp. *That's funny.* So as I was worse in my spirit, I told lies on my roommate in the ministry's home. Because our spirits were growing further apart and he was still praising the Lord at 5:00 a.m., I then heard a voice from God: *I want to talk with you.*

I thought I was losing my mind because the voice would not stop. And then he said that he wanted to talk with me, but I did not have the time. And the next day after this event, I landed a pack-and-load job in the yard of North American Van Lines. I did a high number in dollars, which was $350 in one day. And on top of that, I had about $474 at hand, so we all know what time it was.

What time is it? It's time to partttyyy. And I needed a 3.5 for starters and more and drinks and girls and more than I could handle. Then after four hard days of partying, my heart felt weak, and I felt it slowing down then stopped. I was gone in the floor of the ministry house. I had made it back there before dying.

I ended up in a place of power down on my knees, and I knew who it was in front of myself. And God's power was so great that it was no need to explain because he knows everything. This was the power that I felt, and I was on my way to hell. And the only thing that I could say was, "YOU'RE WORTHY. YOU'RE WORTHY."

You're worthy to be praised, and God started my heart one more time. Now when I got up, I was the happiest soul that had ever lived on the planet Earth. I know this gospel from the front to the back, and it was because of joy. I ended up at Pastor Glendy's Saturday-morning fellowship, and two people or volunteers were needed to stand for testimonies. I stood in a hurry with urgency and excitement because I was overjoyed with love, hope, happiness, and God Almighty.

I had recited Ephesians 6:10–20, which was "The armor of God," word for word like if I had studied it for memory. Then everyone was wondering who I was because this spirit made me look different. I just didn't look the same or feel the same. My thinking wasn't the same.

Then after three months, someone had convinced me that it was just a dream and that I was under the influence of drugs so I need to snap out of it. I had developed a disbelief with this almighty episode. I then relapsed. But I had to leave Orlando because I ran into a street thug named Makeveli. And he like or loved to pistol-whip anyone that he saw selling drugs, mainly other drug dealers. But he wanted to pistol-whip me because he had heard that I thought that I was the baddest.

The Dragon Speaks: Wisdom Is a Defense and Money

Now back at the OK Corral in Tampa where Bean was and was the reason I had left Tampa in the first place. And thinking what would or could happen running into Bean could be a disaster. So I decided to go back to Deeper Life Ministry with Bishop M. B. Jefferson and hide, not knowing what I wanted to do but what I had to do under his leadership.

So instead of me going out to do fundraising with his other pastors, teachers and preachers, I decided to go on my own. I would buy these giant watermelon lollipops where I got thirty-six in a box for $12.99 and made $400 by just having something in my hand. I gave the ministry half of everything that I made, so I was able to look the part. I had a thousand-dollar wardrobe that made me look almost as good as Bishop Jefferson himself. That caused a lot of jealousy in the ministry.

Pastor Ivan came to me one day and stated that I had told the ministry that I said he did not have the Holy Ghost. I really thought that this was too stupid to entertain, but I said, "Yes, I said it." Then Pastor Ivan asked me if I was going to be in bishop's class tonight, and I asked, "Why?"

Pastor Ivan states, "Because I am going to charge you in front of the bishop and class tonight."

I then asked him, "Do you know what to bring?"

Pastor Ivan stated, "Yes, you just bring yourself."

And I said to him, "You don't know what to bring, so I'm going to show you what to bring, and you don't have the Holy Ghost."

I walked into the classroom that evening with $259 in a clear baggy, wanting everyone to see what I had walking up to the bishop. And bishop said, "Speak, my son."

So I said, "Bishop, the Lord anointed me this morning to bring you an offering."

So as the bishop looked around, he again said, "Speak, my son."

"So I went to the corner of Nebraska and Fletcher and was standing on the median. Then a police officer stopped and asked me what I was doing. And I told him that I was waiting on him to give my bishop an offering. So the officer told me to wait over at the gas station, and so I went over to the station, and he bought me $50 for you. Then I went down Fletcher and left on Florida to collect this $259 offering for you."

The bishop looked around and said, "That's what I'm talking about right there."

Then Pastor Ivan ran up to the bishop putting $20 on his desk and bad-mouthing me, and the bishop said, "Don't you ever say anything bad about my son again. Do you hear me? And I'm talking to everyone." I told Pastor Ivan after the class, "I told you that you didn't know what to bring."

Then the next month, I went up to the bishop for a healing of this spirit of deception, so the bishop laid his hands on me, and the dragon speaks. He was talking in another language, and I don't know what he was saying, but the bishop said that I could take that spirit with me because he had never heard a spirit like this one before.

So everyone in the church had something to laugh at about me. *And you can take that spirit with you*, is all I heard. Then bishop-designate Brown had told Bishop Jefferson that I was preaching strange-fire something that sounded like the devil. So we had a meeting in the bishop's office about me leaving the ministry, and I said to Bishop M. B. Jefferson, "Give me seven days to do stone-cold hustling."

I brought a lot of money to this ministry, and I need seven days to leave. So Bishop Jefferson said, "I'll give you seven days to come and go as you please. And keep all that you have as a blessing from me." Everyone was in shock. I started working ten hours per days bringing $400–600 daily.

Then after five days, bishop-designate Brown called me into his office and said, "We made a mistake, so hand over that $3,700 to the ministry." I thought he had lost his mind because he was the one with all the strange-fire rumors.

The Love of My Life

In 2007, I had moved into Loving Hearts Ministry under the leadership of Pastor Knight living in a two-man room with Brother Virgil. I had told Brother Virgil of the things that I've seen and the plans that I had. We would talk for days and all night about ministry and about coming up from the bottom and that I fundraised and was a teacher and preacher under the teachings of Bishop M. B. Jefferson.

Then after resting for two weeks, Pastor Knight decides to send me out with his lead man named Horse, knocking on doors asking for work, but I decided to put on a white shirt and tie asking for money toward the ministry so that we wouldn't come back empty-handed. I had received over a hundred dollars on my first day out, and Pastor Knight immediately made me his lead man.

This made Horse very upset, basically with me. And with a five-man crew, everyone was asked to follow my lead, but no one other than myself was a people person, so I had to do it by myself, and eventually, Pastor Knight was my driver.

I bought five different religious hats. All of them said something different from each other. I asked Pastor Knight to pick one, so he picked the FBI hat, which meant Firm Believer In Jesus. I went from buying a dozen to cases paying $240 for 144 hats and making over $1,000 a case.

Then as time went on, there it was again. Jealousy was in the house coming from the head to the tail. I talked with Brother Virgil about everything plus the jealousy that was in everyone's spirit in the house, so he suggested that I should get prepared to move on to bigger and better things.

Then one hot day with the temperature over ninety-five degrees, Pastor Knight had me working to take his wife to lunch. He had me in Net Park at noon bringing me a box of M&M's, a forty-eight pack, with me handing him over one hundred dollars. I said to him that it was too hot to continue in this heat, but he said that he was taking his wife to lunch.

Then I asked him, "What about the mule?" water on a day like this. But he drove off laughing about my comment about bringing water for the mule. I left Net Park on the no. 41 bus to see Mr. Caldwell that was the owner of these apartments down the street from our ministry. And Mr. Caldwell had purchased cases of my hats at one time and was my friend.

So I sat in his office talking to him about a deal on some hats, but he said, "Will, what do you need? I will give to you freely. Pick out any apartment of mine that you like, and pay me when you can." So I went back that evening to see Pastor Knight, and he plus three other men were waiting on me and said, "Will, you just don't get along with everyone, and you're disobedient to me and this ministry. Now tell me what happened to you today, and where is my money?"

So I stated to the group, "When the mule is worked under the plow, give him water. I have brought thousands to this ministry, and all that I have received is jealousy and hate. Now I'm going to get on the phone and call someone and ask who would like to pick up a grand negro as myself."

Then Pastor Knight screamed, "Get out!" Then I said that my bags are already packed.

I called a girlfriend of mine named Diana to pick me up out of her sleep, and she was mad as hell with a rag around her head talking shit. "Stop it," I said to her, "and act like you're happy to see me, all the money I have put into your pockets." I was on a roll with anyone talking shit to me this day because God had shown up and showed out. So she took me to my apartment that Mr. Caldwell had given me with no money down, and I had enough money to buy all the furniture that I needed.

Two days had gone by, and as I was watching television on a Christian station, a pastor was preaching hard with his wife standing in back of him. And I wondered but found out shortly that she was the real preacher, and right then, I said, "That's the kind of woman I want."

So while I was at UATC bus station, a woman started preaching to me. She was 5'11", a redbone with hazel eyes, and a figure like Jayne Kennedy in her younger days. And she had preached to me for over thirty minutes, and I don't think that I heard a word that she said.

But I did hear when she asked me for $50 for the good word that she had given, and it was for her child, so I gave her my address and said, "Preacher, if you knock on my window at eight tonight with some red thongs in your hand, I will give you $50."

I laughed when I left because she almost had me, so I went home and was watching TV and heard a knock. That's strange because no one knew where I lived. Then I looked out of the window and saw some red thongs waving in my face. Then the preacher lady, Olive, said, "I want my $50."

We didn't leave the apartment for three days. We were married in thirty days, and then she wanted a divorce. She was from Jamaica and was here on a visa. I later relapsed and picked up an attempted-murder charge and was in jail for five and a half months.

Locked Up

In 2008, I started doing furniture at Atlas Van Lines doing pack and load for dispatcher out of New York. And her name was Ms. A-1, doing a man's job, and she was proven. And knowing this, I needed to come plus always have my A game in running. One day, Anita, Ms. A-1, needed a packer on the job at a house off the bus line, and no one had transportation at the time, but I said that I could make it there ASAP.

So I caught the bus off Dale Mabry North as far as it would go, and then I hitched a ride to the destination or house. I padded the front living room and den room furniture in less than one hour. The driver, dispatcher, and shipper were very impressed, and the dispatcher made me her no. 1 patch and loader. Then out of the clear blue, I got locked up for the attempted murder of my wife Olive.

I could change anything, and maybe this was the best thing for me because I didn't have a monkey on my back but a seven-headed dragon, and being locked up was the best time to pray and ask God to set me free. So I prayed, studied, praised, and worshipped.

Then one day, someone asked me to help them with the love or learning the love of God because we do not know how to do time. Some of them had ten to twenty or twenty to life, and they had believed that God had sent me to show them how to do time. At the time, I was "a great show," and the one thing that I knew about being locked up was, *you can be anything that you want.* So I became the greatest show on earth.

I was placed in a single man's cell on the second floor with the shower next door to me, and this one brother stated even when we were released about one sermon that I preached, and the title of that sermon was "Lo-de Bar."

David sends for Mephibosheth, which was in a worthless place and also in mind. Mephibosheth had stated himself that he was nothing but a dead dog. I could relate knowing that the change needed to start from the inside or the spirit of man. And David started showing kindness.

Family, I needed my family, starting with my wife, so I started writing letters of apology and how this change can be made, no answers back, but I believed that the Lord was going to make a way. I got out after five and a half months from being locked up and still had the apartment that Mr. Caldwell gave me.

I went back to it and opened the door and saw that I had been robbed. What happened to all my furniture, and where is my wife? Rob, who worked for Mr. Caldwell, said that she backed up a truck, which belonged to my friend Greg. Greg helped her load up everything and left. Then the neighbor told me that they gave my wife and some young twenty-year-old a ride to church. And the young kid asked my wife when he could move in with her. She told the boy, "My husband would murder you."

Anyway, she filed a restraining order and domestic violence charge against me to receive her citizenship. Then a couple weeks later, she got on the bus with me, and she was talking about how I made her love me, so I knew that she was out of her mind worse than me.

I was so upset about whatever I didn't know, but something was driving me to get high when I didn't want to, and this power was too great for me to handle. So I knew that this dragon had some kind of control over my spirit man, and it will call me at a drop of a hat, and I would answer. But there is one thing that I knew, and that was, *I was alive for a reason.* And it wasn't for the purpose of serving the "son of the devil" even though I was serving him well.

I was dressing up every morning looking like a Sunday morning for breakfast, with flyers in hand with a pastor's name. It was Bishop Keith Irons. As long as I bought him $40–50 daily, it didn't matter what was going on in my life. Up and down the highways, I made two, three, and sometimes four hundred daily, and 70 percent always went to my habit.

Then as time or years went on, I was truly the seven-headed dragon. The son of the devil was living in me, and I couldn't stop him, but I prayed and believed *that one day, the Lord will deliver me.*

Feed the Family

In the year 2010, Tyrone, a one-time friend of mine, came to me with an offer from the queen of marriage, which was for $5,000 to marry a Jamaican girl named Judith and a bonus with the family. But Judith and family didn't know of the habit that I had because of my looks and the conversation on plans that I had for their daughter and the money that was needed for transportation.

Judith was also here on a visa and was an Ohio State University student that ran out of time. And It didn't last any longer than three months before this dragon showed up, and everything changed. Judith tried to hide my madness from her family but couldn't because the money ran out after five months of marriage.

So I would go out to Brandon, Riverview, and other parts of Florida receiving donations, but that was only a starter. I would always let Judith hold a couple hundred dollars and would make her promise not to give it back no matter what I would say. But I would come back so viciously that it frightened her so bad that she was a nervous basket case.

And then we would call her family to bring me some more damn money. And this went on for years, and I threatened her about not telling her family about my condition that I had a large crack habit and was crazy. Then after three and a half years, Judith hadn't received her citizenship from being married to me, and time was up. I needed $5,000 today.

Call your mother, father, sisters, and brothers because I need my money yesterday. I started talking to Judith and her family out of the side of my neck. Then I didn't care what they had thought about me. She moved out, and I couldn't get her back. Man, what a great woman she was, and I miss her even today.

In 2013, I moved on 22nd Live Oak Landings, and they welcomed me. I was in the HUD-VASE program and only paid third of what I made. And I started working at Tampa General through 717 Parking. Then after two years of trying to get my act together, if that's what we want to call it, I spoke to a manager's daughter that didn't look like the best-looking girl.

I said, "What a beautiful day for a beautiful person."

She said, "OH, you want to be funny. I'll be back, motherf——." So her mother named Cookie that was a supervisor walked over to me, and I said, "Don't do it, you little midget." She was younger than me and was about 4'11" but hit me with a three-punch combo.

Then she said, "Come on, you motherf——!" And she was too fast for me, and I couldn't see me taking another combo from that New Yorker. So I walked over to the police on duty and said, "That midget tried to kill me."

The police laughed and said, "Are there any witnesses?"

I said, "The camera."

The hospital fired her and then me because I was a threat to the hospital or a liability, and who cares? It wasn't enough money anyway. The hundred in gratuities and only getting $600 every two weeks was something that I owe out when I got paid. And I had bigger fish to fry.

Bound for five years, after the job at the hospital, I started doing donations for anybody and mainly myself and then boosting at a number of stores, like Best Buy and Walmart. Then a girl named CC introduced me to a dealer named Mean. and I wondered about that name, but someone found out why he was called Mean.

But just meeting him, I had convinced him that I was a big money spender and needed someone with some weight because of my habit. So he gave me by just meeting him $275 of credit, and the next day, he sent his boys around to collect his money. I had his $275 plus some, and he was more than surprised, and I was loyal to Mean, and no one could do no wrong to me.

Ms. El's boyfriend that was larger than me and younger by thirty years and was named Animal wanted to whip me because I had taken one thousand dollars out of Ms. El's mouth, but Mean heard about it. The next time I saw Animal, he was a Chihuahua with no bite.

So I watched "Live Oak" for Mean, and every transaction had to come through me. And if whomever didn't want to act accordingly, Mean would take the money and give a crumb then the pack of crack to me. Then he would make his statement: "The next time, give all the money to Main Man."

Main Man was the nickname that Mean had given me, and it was because of a number of other things in being loyal to him. Mainly, it was because I always and never missed giving him his money. And the party's people with money always came to my house for whatever was needed. *I had it* or was going to get it.

Then when I would close shop for a couple of days wanting to quit mainly because God was convicting me, Mean would always make me open my door and say, "You must be sick. Here, Main Man, this is what you need." And he would always set out three large stones, and I would smoke them then call him back to get ready.

And whatever I needed for the party or just something to hold, he never had a problem with it. As the years went by, everything started going bad. It was mainly my spirit man, and I realize that I was being loyal to the devil, and someone had told me something one day that was true, which was, "the dangerous man in the world is illiteracy."

No wonder he was mean to everyone except for me, but really, Mean introduced me to all his friends as Main Man and being no. 1 on his team. Riding with Mean was the last time because he said, "Let's take a ride." So we did. And down the road we went, and he showed me the weight we were riding with.

Then he said going through Sulphur Springs and driving fast, "If the police gets behind us, I'm going to bend around a corner in high speed. You open the door with this key of dope, and don't forget to roll when you jump out of the car to the ground, and I'll come back to get you later, or go to the house."

But it never happened. The police was never around on this ride. And I was never nervous, but this time, I was. We were pulling up in dark places behind so-called abandoned houses with only candles for lights. And at every house, each person was coming out handing Mean $800 or better. I realized that everyone that knew him gave him the name Mean.

In 2017, Mean put Soldier Boy in my apartment to sell, but Mean had to pay me because Soldier Boy didn't know how because in every hundred dollars, I was required $25 in my house, but Soldier Boy had another plan. He started giving me credit, and I let him but also said that I didn't pay for credit in my house.

And because Soldier Boy felt that I owed him $90 and he wasn't going to get paid, he decided to call over one at his boys to take over my apartment. So they talked in the front room of my apartment all night about their takeover. And with my bedroom door locked, I had called my play brother, James.

James was 270 lbs. and had been to prison eleven different times and didn't play the radio. So when James came over in the morning, I opened the door, and he came in stating that everyone had five minutes to pack and leave. Then Soldier Boy disputed with him about having nothing to do with this. But James stated, "Will is my brother." Then when Soldier Boy didn't want to listen, James grabbed his own Johnson and screamed at the top of his lungs: *You got the right motherf—— now!*

And he backed Soldier Boy down the sidewalk around the apartments and rental office. Everyone including the office management saw and heard the drama, which was a class act to never forget. And after this performance, I was asked to leave. The manager said that they wouldn't renew my lease or accept any more payments from me or HUD-VASE.

Chapter 11

In March 2017, I ended up still in HUD-VASE and on 46th and Sewaha Street, the Arms Apartments. I was counseled about not answering or opening my door because of the activities and people. I stated that I swear those acts will never happen again. Then the next day after I had moved in, I had received a phone call from management.

And the office manager stated, "On camera, we have never seen as much drug activity and drama in all the history of this apartment. We want you to leave, Mr. Hagwood." And I promise again that this could never happen again. I just didn't know. And at apartment number four, where I was, they had just been busted for selling drugs. So they asked, "Do I understand?" And of course, I said, "I do."

I promised myself, plus I really meant it also and went outside of my door looking to the left of me. Upstairs, it was "Grand Central Station." So I asked about upstairs, about apartment nineteen, and it was said that that was Dorset's place. Anything that I needed was at apartment nineteen. So I had Fred to introduce me to Dorset, and we had become friends, and he invited me to this set.

"Sit down, and get comfortable. What would you like to drink?" With my feet up and looking around seeing four giant lodge couches and a giant couch for relaxation, Dorset explained his set and the people in it for business and pleasure. The girls, if they wanted anything, had to get naked and get busy. "It's time to go to work, and go get some money, plus when you come back, baby, Daddy's going to take care of you."

My setup was totally different because I had become homicidal and suicidal. And I started keeping the same kind of company day after day and night after night and ended up in the VA's ARC seven times in 2017. At one time, I sent my play brother, James, over to my apartment to put out the "riffraff."

Then getting out of the ARC in January 2018, I had those same "riffraff" come to my apartment to sell and party. As time passed by, remembering the bad things came up often, like the time I sent James over to put everyone out of my house. At the time, I had a so-called dope dealers named "Trick and Turtle" in my apartment. These two were the worst of the worst, and I had them together.

As time went on, I was working for Turtle and wondered how this happened. So one day, Turtle handed me three bags and said for me to make his money. So I called the police and said, "I'm a White boy over at the Arms, and I just got jumped by five brothers." The police where there in five minutes and put everyone out of my apartment.

Then they asked me where the White boy was, and I said, "That's me. I'm the White boy, and I need a ride because I fear for my life." So the police searched me before giving me a ride and didn't find anything.

I had drugs up under my testicles in my underwear. I was asked by a very-nice officer where I needed to go and be dropped off at. Then I said, "Over Ray's house," and Ray lived on the other side of town, and he would possibly be the only friend that would let me in with my stolen drugs.

Meanwhile, talking to the officer and going down the road, I had told him to go back to the apartment complex to find Turtle. I know that he is still in the area and possibly in one of the neighbor's apartment. And I want the police to apprehend Turtle because I had his drugs and was going over Ray's to finish it off. When I got there, I told Ray everything that had happened and said, "Things don't look good for me, so what should I do?"

"Wait just a minute. I know what to do!" Ray said.

"Let's smoke some crack, and I have three bags. Remember?"

But Ray didn't want any of it, and he said later that someone needed to have a clear head. And I didn't have a clear head or conscience. Then as I was pulling out the bags, my vision started going blurry, having rocks all on the floor and under the chairs. I told Ray that I have been up for too many days drugging, and my mind plus my body was starting to shut down.

As we talked, I fell asleep and woke up after ten hours, and Ray had left the house. Then there was a knock on the door. It was one of Ray's girlfriends. Then as soon as we started getting high, she got so nervous of me that she ran out the door.

Nothing but the Truth

In early 2018, I, William Hagwood, was moved into the seven-headed dragon's backyard. It was through again the HUD-VASE program at Palms Garden on 122nd St. and FL Ave., which was where I had met Sandy and Jay Rock. Sandy was seven months pregnant and needed a stable place to live other that a hotel night after night and day after day. So I moved in this so-called happy couple in my front room for the exchange of a fifty rock daily.

So after two days, I had brought my partner, Amos, alias "Flavor Flav" because he looked exactly like Flavor Flav and probably got high alike. "I'm just saying, not sure."

And I had talked Amos into spending over $400 with Jay Rock only and didn't get paid for my service. So this started the first fight but not the last over drug and drug money in my apartment, and this wasn't going to be the last. And through our fighting, I had learned that the drugs that Jay Rock had were given to him by Sandy. And to make things all right, Sandy decided to compensate me for an additional week that made Jay Rick thirty-eight hot.

Now Jay Rock at the age of twenty-four wanted me to run with Sandy and from my house, wanting some reimbursement money from them because he was ready to leave. And Jay Rock said to Sandy, "Let's go," and Sandy said, "I ain't going anywhere." She went to the bedroom and closed the door to lay down. Then I and Jay Rock looked at each other. Then I said, "I guess she's running things," and he left.

So now it was no one but me, Sandy, and the baby on the way, one little happy family. "WAKE UP. WAKE UP!"

But Sandy would make up every morning screaming, "Where is my drugs? There's no one in the apartment but me and you. Will, so you're stealing." So I ended up being pimped by Sandy in my own apartment and needed to pay her every day for something that I didn't do. Then having another conversation with Jay Rock, he had told me that Sandy did him the same way and she smokes rocks even with the baby.

Jay Rock also said, "Then she told me that he was glad that I wanted her and that her grandmother studies voodoo. It's a religion practiced chiefly in Haiti and the Haitian diaspora. Practitioners are called 'voodooists' or 'servants of the spirits.' And the followers can be mainly found in Jamaica, and Sandy is Jamaican and already has a spell on you!"

Now at the apartment, Sandy looked at me and said that I've been talking with Jay Rock, but how did she know? Then she cursed with words that could only be from Satan, stating me and Jay Rock were "dick in the booty-ass nig——," and asked me what we were really talking about, and I started walking away from the apartment because Sandy was making me nervous. I ended up in the VA's ARC.

I stated to the nurse in the ER that I was suicidal and homicidal and ready to take my own life and had a hex on me believing that Sandy was a witch. Then after three days, I was released from the hospital and back at my apartment to find a short midget named Mookie that waved a pistol around only being eighteen years old and was Sandy's new lover and was sleeping in my bed in my apartment.

But it was another way of looking at this situation, and believe it or not, these two were so much in love that they were slipping. So when they were asleep at night, I sold their drugs, crack and heroine, like I wanted to. And I would turn in half the money and still wanted my house cut, making Mookie too upset. So I left the apartment because Mookie was getting or was under a spell from Sandy and was like a chicken with his head cut off.

And while at the VA's ARC two times in a row, I would call the police, telling them about Mookie to get him out of my apartment, and finally, it worked. Mookie was taken or picked up by his supplier because he was losing too much money under Sandy's control. It was because Sandy was in her eight month having Mookie whopped under her spell and drove out of his mind. "Damn, I don't want to see none of that."

Anyone Will Do

Now myself and Sandy were looking good. At least, I thought so until a Spanish thief named Angel came to my door. He had a $2000 racing bike, and all that was needed for him was $75, so Sandy paid the $75. Then I took the bike to Max Pawn Shop to receive $200 then brought it to Sandy. Then Sandy gave me a hundred in rocks and a Spanish girl named April.

After things were going well with boosting for clothes to fit Sandy and myself, there was a knock at the door. It was an undercover police with a warrant because of the bike, and now I was locked up.

Maybe it was or I know that it was a great thing that happened at the time because it was God's perfect will. And I know that when we try to do good, evil follows, and when we do bad, God always brings us back.

I was worried about Sandy and the baby mainly because Sandy was smoking too much. She would put on the pipe about a twenty piece with fire in the dark, and all you could see was her eyes looking like the dragon the day that he was born. So I believe that she was where I was, in the devil's adversary, and anyone will do.

I started studying; praising the Lord; playing chess, which I called the game of life; and exercising daily. I couldn't sleep mainly because the matts were only one-inch thick. So I went to see the doctor about getting a double mat plus pain pills for sleep and my back.

The doctor said, "Okay," then wrote me a prescription, which said, "Stay out of jail. This place isn't for your comfort. The one-inch mats are for a purpose so that you think about this the next time you decide to commit a crime."

The doctor was so right, and that was a lesson I'll never forget, some real medicine. In studying God's work and having a study group, I made a statement, which was, "I'm content right here and now by just learning, breathing, and my spirit man being lifted up. My destiny is to be a jailhouse preacher," and at that moment, a voice came over the intercom: "William Hagwood, pack it up."

I was just bonded out by Mean's lieutenant named Doug, sir name "New York," but only to use my apartment, seeing the great business that was happening while locked up for three and a half weeks. And Sandy was still there, so when we got to my apartment, Sandy was telling New York how rotten I was, making him upset and then saying to Sandy, "Get your shit, and get the f—— out. I know Will. This is 'Main Man,' the name given by Mean."

The Best Time I Ever Had

So the crew came, and it was about eighteen crew members. Everyone coming to the spot had to show love to Main Man, orders from Mean to York and everyone, and I was boosting, bringing the whole crew new items daily. But all in all, they were feeding me about $350 in drugs a day and buying me with drugs and any woman of my desire.

Then I had met this young Spanish girl with a black eye and only thirty-three years old, and she was in a fight, so I invited her over to fix herself up. Her name was Jenny, and she had a walk that shook the world.

I was really friends with Jenny then wondered why she was with a boyfriend that beat her up. And she said that his name was Angel and he was locked up, but it didn't dawn on me at the time that this was the same Angel that sold me the stolen bike.

When Angel got out of jail, he asked me if I had been with his girl, and I said, "Dog, I would never." Then we bump hands and shoulders. Then he went on about his way. Then two weeks went by, and Angel was screaming and banging at my door. "Big Will, I need to talk to you."

I didn't answer the door because I knew what Angel wanted and was upset about. I believe that he said to

Jenny that she wasn't shit and Jenny probably said to him that "that isn't what Big Will said."

I had told Jenny one morning while standing in the mirror that she was truly the best piece of ass that I've ever had in my fifty-nine years of living. And Jenny had smiled that day to be the happiest girl on earth because she knew that I meant it from last night's performance coming from the heart.

I will always remember Jenny, and it reminds me of the movie with Michael Douglas in *Romancing the Stone*. They named a boat called "Jenny."

I ended up going back to the VA's ARC a total of eight times in 2018 trying to get some time with God, some time away from all the madness and back to reality, and the world in the state of things as they exist, as opposed to an idealistic idea of them.

And we as people think of strife as being a part of reality, but no, it is the unreality. So looking in the Bible as being part of my research, I find in Isaiah 6:2 the word *seraphim.*

Seraphim was the four creatures that came forth giving God praise with holy fire and were the burning ones. They were God's champions in giving a lesson to the twenty-four elders in Revelation.

And God decided to give man his very best, which are seraphim that are on our right shoulder today. And Michael the Archangel (meaning chief of angels, highest messenger) was to give the assignment to seraphim.

Strife and this place on earth are on the other side of the wall of time. So we have no excuse knowing that in the book of Peter, God gives us everything to make it. But there is a need to know that strife is unreality.

What about Me?

I had spent a week at the VA's ARC in studying reality and the power of God then blessing plus curses. And I realized that I had caused curses in my life and upon my eternal soul.

Then my name was called to be discharged from the hospital, but I wasn't ready to leave for one reason: I wasn't going back to my apartment on 122nd at Palms Gardens, and the second reason was because I hadn't received my wallet with numbers for a new location or gotten an answer from the SUDS program. I told one of the patient techs that I was not ready to leave and the reason, so he told me to act crazy then they will let me stay.

So I had seen my social worker passing by and said to him that I need my wallet to call for help, and he said that he had other patients. And I screamed at the top of my lungs, "What about meeeeee? What about meeeeee?" I think that I overreacted, and getting everyone's attention, you could have heard a pen drop.

At first, everyone was in a freeze mode (nobody moves; nobody gets hurt). The little skinny social worker was trembling in his shoes as I was looking at him eyeball to eyeball, being too scared to move. Then I heard footsteps running through the hall and coming for me.

When they arrived on the scene, they already had my wallet, clothes, and discharge papers and told me to be off the property as soon as possible. So I called David Smith's office number, and he said for me to come to 46th Street to enter me in the SUDS programs.

You Dumbass

So I was accepted in the A1 twenty-eight-day program and was ready for anything. The rules were no problem. I sat down with Mr. Nat in his office to be interviewed and questioned for success.

Nat asked me, "Are you excited to be here?" and I replied, "Yes, I'm very excited to be here. Thank you."

Then Nat replied, "You still a dumb motherf———."

So I replied with a maybe and proceeded on to the next question about my hobbies, which was chess. I have been in all kinds of competitions for over forty years. And Nat's reply was, "And don't look for anyone here to play your dumbass." I was at a loss for words and self-esteem, so I just listened until the interview was over. Then Nat said, "Take your dumbass to your room."

So at first, I thought that this was the initial intake for the program. Then in the morning, I was late getting to the van, and there was no warning or wake-up call. So Nat sent in one of the clients to tell me, "Nat said for you to bring your stupid ass on, motherfu———."

That was the last straw. Then I caught myself and said, "Wait, and be patient." At the end of the day, while on 46th Street, I saw David Smith to ask him about the name-calling by Nat, and David did not believe me because Nat was the nicest person that he had ever met. I said to David, "Why would I lie?" and he said, "Addicts lie."

I said to myself, "Ain't this a bitch. I can't win for losing, and every time I think I'm winning, I'm still losing."

Then two weeks later, Drew Park-Act 2 called me.

Surprise

I decided to sign out early two days before Christmas to sign in at Drew Park-Act 2, and Nadia was coming to get me. So everything was working out great knowing that I could do my one-year probation here at the same time.

So I pulled up to Drew Park-Act 2's location with Nadia telling me to park my bags in front of the building where I'll be living. Then something had changed with Nadia, and I couldn't put my finger on it just yet.

Then while sitting, a fellow vet wanted to show me around, so I said, "Okay." But the funny thing about him showing the place and rooms was that he was in a hurry. So he showed me two other rooms that I liked a lot and then showed me the room that was assigned to me. It looked like a crack house room, the worse that I have ever seen. I was in total shock and disbelief.

Then I was told to run over to the office and see Ms. Jane about the condition of the room, but before I could or was about to talk with Ms. Jane, Nadia came boldly to my face saying, "What's wrong with the room?" And she was saying it like I was making things up, so I asked her if she saw the room, and she said, "No." I told her of the bad conditions of the room, and the mattress was drying from pee.

Now having two other rooms available, I would prefer one of them. Then Nadia responded in the nastiest way saying, "You don't run anything nor make any decisions around here. You don't tell us what to do. Do I make myself clear, Mr. Hagwood?" I should have said, "BITCH," with all capital letters.

You can take me back to the place where you, Ms. Nadia, picked me up from, and now do I make myself clear? And so as she went to get the keys to the van, I called Ms. Kiana at Act 1, and she stated that I'm already signed out and said, "Will, you need to apologize because tomorrow is Christmas Eve and nothing will be open."

"Damn, so when I think that, I'm winning, and I'm still losing."

So I went back to the office apologizing stating to Ms. Nadia and Jane that it wasn't that bad and whatever is wrong, I'll make it right. (I was the butt kisser for the year.)

"Please," but it did no good. Nadia said, "You showed your ass in front of my staff and clients, so what would they think letting you get away with your mouth?"

I was speechless and couldn't say a word. So I put my bags on the van to drop them off over a friend's house then got on the HARTline Bus, and the destination was The Good Samaritan, which was the worst place that I should go, but I was broken. And I couldn't live up to the situation or to produce the correct reaction when a heart has been broken. At the same time, I think or know that I had lost respect for myself.

Running for My Life

As I walked through the hallway of The Good Samaritan Inn or the OK Corral, it was the only place that I wasn't barred from or wasn't remembered. But I do remember the last time that I was here. I was running out of the back door stating to Frank that I was going to the laundromat. But the truth of the matter was that I had to get out of town for robbing a drug dealer named Bean.

But this matter was twenty years ago, and who would remember that I took all the child's Christmas toys? No drugs but the Christmas presents because Bean had lied putting a gun in my face.

It was said that Bean was doing life in the penitentiary as a repeat offender, and I need to remind him not to drop the soap.

In the morning on Christmas Day, I woke up on a couch hoping that I didn't contract any bedbugs. So I got up and moved to the hallway hoping for a cup of coffee but ran into an old smoke buddy. I had forgot his name, so I said, "What's going on, White boy? Tell me something good." So he said, "Bean."

"Bean I thought was doing life in the pen?"

He said that Bean was but was released on good behavior.

"Damn, well, where is he?"

And he answered, "Bean is upstairs. Should I go get him for you?"

I answered, "No," while I was shivering in my shoes.

Then a so-called gentleman walked downstairs, and it was Bean. And he looked at me after twenty years of hate then got on the phone. So I ran out the door across the street in traffic almost getting hit but stopping the bus. And with no change, the bus driver gave me a ride seeing the terrified condition I was in. In 2018, on Christmas Day, I was running for my life.

Into Walmart, I went with the mind of believing that this was my store and everything in it. And no one can say anything to me about my things in my store. Then after seven minutes, I was finished and started walking to the door with security meeting me and saying, "Mr. Hagwood, we've been waiting on you."

Then I said to security, "It's about time."

Then they asked me to walk to the office with them, and I did and felt relieved. When we got to the office, I unloaded thirty-four packs of lady's underwear and bras. And I was looked upon with a puzzled and confused look. Then I was asked, "Who was going to wear these items, and for what? And what is on your mind, Mr. Hagwood, because we never sat down with a person as calm as yourself?"

"I've been in your stores four and a half years boosting and selling items back for cash to buy crack cocaine. And today, I'm tired of myself and all my actions. So before I came into your store today, I said in the mighty name of Jesus, 'Deliver me.' Now you can take me to jail."

And the officer that was listening said, "No." Promise me that you'll come to court, and if you promise me, I will believe you and let you go.

On the second of January, I had received a call from Chuck Taylor from Volunteers of America, VOA for short. I moved in a shared two-bedroom apartment with Charles. He was a lifer and in other words would do any low-down scum of a thing till the day he dies for a crumb of crack.

I couldn't win for losing, and every direction was backward; then I got a call from J. Gunzellas at the public defender's office. I was to be in court this coming February to sign contract for veteran court. It was a twelve-month contract being clean and sober, and on completion, all charges will be dropped.

In the Mighty Name of Jesus

I couldn't nor haven't stayed clean any longer than five and a half months in thirty-seven years. I asked J. Gunzellas about time in the penitentiary, but he looked at me with a shitty grin on his face. So leaving downtown, I was getting high, but it wasn't enough. I picked up an order for Sandy by her new boyfriend, a dealer with weight.

Sandy needed some new underclothes and lots of them. And I needed a 3.5 in weight. I needed a 3.4 in crack, and believing that I couldn't be stopped because I had boosted out of Walmart for the past four and a half years, I believed that I won't nor couldn't stop. And before entering the store, I looked up to leave and said, "In the mighty name of Jesus, Lord, deliver me."

The Arms of the Enemy Are Broken

As a soldier, when the presence of the Lord shows up, it's "change." And there's nothing you can do to stop the work of the Lord. Every addiction to personality is broken in the name of Jesus. There's no greater power than the power that's in the Lord's name.

In the mighty name of Jesus, the soldier's said, "The earth shook. That made the stone roll back." And we stood as dead men. Then we saw real power, which was Jesus Christ.

That's why every knee shall bow and every tongue confess that Jesus is Lord.

"Real Soldier Power"

Meaning: are always constantly encouraged to grow in every area of success.

Strategies:

1. Let's pray about a plan to meet our goals.
2. Be sure about our tactics and strategies that we'll use on the battlefield.
3. Most importantly, if any of your fellow soldiers fall, don't push the button. "Go back."

My statement: "There will be no soldiers left behind."

I was in Bible study in Gibsonton, Florida, and the topic was the first people to see Jesus when he rose. The Bible study booklet said that it was the two Mary's, but I stated that I didn't agree, so the teacher asked me in a quizzical way. I stated that it was the soldiers and don't forget about the soldiers that were there.

And I carry that soldier's spirit today, and everyone in that Bible-study class needed for me to prove it, and I did. The pastor said that it would be best if I didn't return because I talk too much.

I had stated that in the four Gospels, it says, "The earth shook, and the stone rolled back, and the soldiers stood as dead men. And the spirit had power that they couldn't compare it to. That they never experience power like this before."

In Matthew 28:11–15, you'll find that these soldiers were walking through the town telling everyone and the elders what had happened. They said, "We saw REAL POWER. STAND UP!"

I'm a thirty-seven-year-old crack addict, and I have never been clean longer than five and a half months, and this was because of being locked up. So I knew the kind of power that was needed. I got up at four in the morning and turned on some gospel music to give God praise.

And this was only a starter. After six months, I got baptized in Jesus's name, and when I came up out of the water, a question was asked: "Do you feel anything that's different?" And I was upset because I didn't feel a thing.

At about noon on a Saturday after I had received the color yellow, for only once a week, I had been thinking about getting high for 188 days, and I was overwhelmed with a powerful spirit that did not care about anything.

And I was going to get high, so I walked to think, and everything that I know and learned didn't matter. So outside on the corner of 19th and Fletcher looking in both directions toward the south and north, I saw dealers in both directions, four to the north and one to south, so I started to walk toward the north.

My legs started to lock up, and I couldn't talk. And I didn't want to get all the way down there in a speechless condition. Then I turned going right and saw two other dealers on bicycles, but I couldn't talk. So I made another right toward the meat market and looked up into the clouds seeing a crack in the sky. "It was the eye of Christ looking down on me."

And then I remembered the soldiers, and the Lord took me back over two thousand years standing with my fellow brothers and soldiers. And we felt "THE EARTH SHOOK AND THE STONE ROLLED BACK." And we saw real power standing, which was Jesus Christ.

Real Charity

"The greatest of all time" is charity because of its scars. "The price for the prize."

MLK was talking about himself or what he could have been if he had accepted the riches of the world, "a fool."

But God said to him, "You fool! This 'very night,' your life is demanded of you. And the things you have prepared, whose will they be?"

That's how it is with the one who stores up treasure for himself and is not rich toward God.

Like anybody, I like to live a long life, but long jeopardy has its place, and I just want to do God's will.

And he allowed me to go up to the mountain. And I looked over "and seen the promise land."

I may not get there with you, but I want you to know "tonight" that we as a people will get to the promise land.

So tonight, "I'm not worried about anything nor fearing any man."

My eyes have seen the glory of the coming of the Lord.

That's charity.

My brother, John, asked me to pray for him because he was in a suicide condition. Was he a true believer? I give you all the Jesus that I have.

"That's real charity."